# Public Speaking

*10 Simple Methods to Build Confidence, Overcome Shyness, Increase Persuasion and Become Great at Public Speaking*

*Public Speaking*

**PUBLISHED BY: James W. Williams**
**Copyright © 2018 All rights reserved.**

No part of this publication may be copied, reproduced in any format, by any means, electronic or otherwise, without prior consent from the copyright owner and publisher of this book.

# Contents

Introduction ............................................................. 6

Chapter 1 ................................................................. 9

Understanding the Context of Public Speaking .. 9

Chapter 2 ................................................................ 16

Building Confidence ............................................... 16

    Positive Mental Image ..................................... 18

    Visualizing public speaking success ............... 20

    Slay the inner critic .......................................... 21

    Develop a fearless stage persona .................... 22

    Mix the ingredients up ..................................... 23

Chapter 3 ................................................................ 24

Speech Creation and Delivery ............................... 24

    Vocal Preparation ............................................. 33

Chapter 4 ................................................................ 34

10 Simple Methods to Public Speaking Mastery 34

    Unleash the Inner Master ................................ 34

    Practice the Art of Story Telling ..................... 35

Focus on the audience and ignite a conversation .................................................... 36

Deliver Captivating Moments ......................... 37

Grab attention and close with dynamic end ... 37

Stick to 18-Minute Rule ................................. 38

Engage all the 5 Senses ................................... 39

Study the Masters .......................................... 39

Let your personality shine through ................ 40

Fail Forward ................................................... 41

Chapter 5 ........................................................... 42

Developing Persuasion Skills ............................ 42

Conclusion ........................................................ 46

Thank you! ........................................................ 48

## Your Free Gift

As a way of saying thanks for your purchase, I wanted to offer you a free bonus E-book called ***Bulletproof Confidence Checklist*** exclusive to the readers of this book.

To get instant access just go to:

https://theartofmastery.com/confidence/

Inside the book, you will discover:

- What is shyness & social anxiety, and the psychology behind it
- Simple yet powerful strategies for overcoming social anxiety
- Breakdown of the traits of what makes a confident person
- Traits you must DESTROY if you want to become confident
- Easy techniques you can implement TODAY to keep the conversation flowing
- Confidence checklist to ensure you're on the right path of self-development

# Introduction

If you have ever listened to a great speaker then you can attest to the fact that there's something that's not only inspiring but also uplifting when sitting before a poised and polished public speaker. Public speaking may come naturally for some but it's also an art that can be learned and mastered. Mastering public speaking is beneficial in diverse ways as it precipitates self-discovery, builds confidence and also triggers self-expression.

Effective communication skill is considered as the backbone of the society and can be used to influence decisions, form connections and motivate change. Effective speaking enhances one's ability to progress in their personal and work life. Great public speaking is a skill that every business person should consider developing in this competitive environment. It takes great speaking and persuasion skills to gain customers attention for increased sales and business growth.

As much as public speaking may come naturally to some, the fear of public speaking is one of the common phobias that many people contend with on a daily basis. It's a kind of performance anxiety that can be quite paralyzing but the good news is that whether public speaking comes to you naturally or you feel a rise in anxiety whenever you're faced with an opportunity to speak publicly; the principles shared in this book has the potential of transforming you into a world class speaker.

There are loads of information on public speaking that have been shared. However, finding a resource that takes you through a step-by-step process from a state of fear and anxiety in public speaking to a state where you get to hear applause from the audience after delivering a speech is what this book focuses on. **Public Speaking: 10 Simple Methods to Build Confidence, Overcome Shyness, Increase Persuasion and Become Great at Public Speaking** is a book that has covered in detail what it takes to become a great public speaker.

The book has shared in-depth insight on understanding the context of public speaking, building confidence, speech creation, vocal preparation and all that you need to do in order to become a great speaker. You also get to learn the 10 simple methods that you can use to build confidence and influence effectively and become a master at public speaking. Whether you are already a pro at public speaking or you are just getting started; there are valuable nuggets in this book that can help you with your journey to becoming great at public speaking.

# Chapter 1

# Understanding the Context of Public Speaking

Ideas are considered as the currency of the 21st century and public speaking is critical if one is to succeed in selling their ideas persuasively. Communications in its various forms pervades the current business environment as much as many people tend to overlook the importance of effective communication. With many people struggling with insecurity about public speaking; having knowledge of what it takes to deliver a great presentation can be liberating. Once you master the art of public speaking, you will be more confident in your abilities to deliver a more dynamic presentation and fire up your audience in a way that they find to be irresistible.

Public speaking cover a wide genre such as facilitating a meeting, stage presentations, interviews, training sessions, arguments, answering questions, negotiations, making calls, working with clients and more. Whether your focus is in enhancing your professional growth, inspire and persuade your audience to take some action or even take your business to the next level; you need ways that you can use to convey your ideas in a more clear, captivating and structured way. Regardless of your level of communication skills, you can become more confident, more impressive and more competent as a speaker.

Speaking can be viewed in two parts, creating a talk and performing a talk. Creating a talk entails everything you do before you speak while performing a talk entails everything that you do as you engage in speaking. Effective communication is therefore achievable when one manages to master both the two parts. One may be a great speech writer but lacks the confidence to say what they have written. Another person may also be comfortable with speaking but lacks valuable things to talk about. One may also think that they are great at both even as their audience strongly disagree. Regardless of your skill level, you can still improve in your public speaking skills.

Most people can clearly remember listening to a person giving a great speech or presentation however, it becomes harder to identify and even synthesize the elements that constitute a powerful speech. There are various factors that constitutes to a great speech; it could be because the topic being discussed is of interest to the listeners. It could also be that the speaker is authentic and engaging. An authentic public speaker can be perceived as engaging in ways that surpasses the context of the subject in discussion and that can in turn give the message an element of significance that it might have lacked.

Learning how to speak and being able to present authentically with the intention of conveying to the audience the information at hand is critical. In order to bring out a more authentic self in delivering a great speech consider the following;

## Understand the Context

Context refers to the actual space that you are to speak in. You should be able to understand your audience and be able to gauge beforehand their interests. Public speaking requires that you have an audience that's willing to listen and also engage with you. Carrying out an audience analysis will in turn lead to igniting greater audience interest, improved credibility towards the speaker, and a more receptive audience.

## Be Yourself

We are all different and unique in our ways and to be authentic, you have to know how to be yourself whenever you're in the spotlight. Trying to imitate someone will only make you display an uncomfortable body language that might not be consistent with what you're saying. Avoid emulating the techniques used by others and instead let your experiences and personality guide you as you present. In doing so, you will be making the right steps in ensuring that your listeners are receptive and are also willing to consider thoughtfully the content of your presentation.

## Understand your topic

There are different contexts of public speaking and despite the circumstances you find yourself in, it's advisable that you have good understanding of the topic that you intend to speak about. When you have understanding, you will then focus less on thinking about what to communicate and how to engage with the audience. The more time you spend with your content for better understanding the more confident you will be while speaking on the topic.

## Never be afraid to improvise

Regardless of how well you plan, things may not turn out exactly as you had planned. Public speaking can at times be unpredictable right from the faulty projectors to last minute changes. A public speaker should be able to improvise whenever something turns out in an unexpected way. It could be a malfunction of the presentation equipment which makes it impossible to display visuals. It could be a question from the audience that you're unsure of how to answer. You don't have to sweat, just develop some composure and try to be flexible so as to think of ways to improvise.

**Play to your strengths**

People are gifted differently; there are those who are great story tellers. There are also those capable of bringing life into any raw information they speak about. Others are great at using their body language and mannerisms to ignite engagement with the audience. Just know that there is no right or wrong ways to deliver a speech. Great speakers are capable of identifying their strengths and using them as tools to create a presence that's relatable and authentic. While preparing to deliver a speech, you also need to determine ways that you can use your strengths to connect with the audience and you will come out as a more authentic speaker.

## Benefits of developing effective public speaking skills

- Creates opportunities for career growth
- Positions one as an authority in a given field.
- Provides an edge above the competition
- Ability to market products and services to larger audiences effectively
- Ability to assume leadership and impact others
- Motivates and persuades others to attain professional goals and take relevant actions.

## Chapter 2

# Building Confidence

Confidence is one of the most important attributes that you can have as a public speaker. It is an overarching attitude, a feeling about oneself that enables one to speak with an assured sense of authenticity. With confidence, one is able to see the best of every situation in a clear context. One is able to trust their public speaking abilities and also feel in control of the situation. A lack of confidence stem from an individual's early development. It also comes from the childhood experiences and the way in which you remember them. To build confidence, one has to be ready to change their behaviors which in turn change the signals to your brain that affirm your value and self worth.

Being fearless as a public speaker entails a mix of both passion and authenticity. To be confident as a public speaker, you need to ask yourself a few questions such as "How can I become fearless as a public speaker? How can I become confident in public speaking? When your adrenaline sets in and you become nervous, it affects one's ability to act normal. Building confidence entails being able to get through public speaking without showing the audience that you're nervous. Most public speakers struggle and stress over trying to be fearless and confident irrespective of how they feel inwardly.

They in the process fall into the trap of pushing the nerves away to express a feeling of being confident. What happens as one struggle to push away the fears is that they end up sabotaging themselves and in turn fails to connect with the audience. Powerful public speaking may start with talking from the heart even if you are not 100% confident. Instead of pushing the feelings of fear away, you can find a way of using the energy for good. Being fearless as a public speaker is not necessarily a lack of fear; it's more about taking the fear and transforming it into energy and excitement around your message.

To build confidence in public speaking, you can follow the below steps;

## Positive Mental Image

Psychologists have stated that those who are deeply confident as public speakers tend to have a positive mental imagery that reinforces confidence. If your mental imagery expresses lack of confidence then that's what reflects in your speaking. To develop a positive mental image;

- Practice picturing yourself speaking. Look out for the senses that get stimulated. What do you hear, smell or see? Do you feel nervous or confident? What is it in your mental imagery that makes you feel that way?

- Play the positive mental image of you speaking and picture yourself looking from out of your body. Try to change the colors of the room where you're speaking and see what happens to your level of confidence. How do you see the audience? Are they sitting or standing? Are they close or a bit far? Adjust the audience the way you want in your mental image until you begin to feel confident and powerful.

- Are there people in the audience that are not receptive? Picture them with some clown nose and see if it makes you feel more confident. It may sound inappropriate but just do it anyway.

- Feel the reaction of the audience. Do you hear silence or laughter? Picture a firm grounding of the floor in your mental imagery, something that will make you feel more confident.

- Practice these shifts mentally whenever you think of giving a speech. The practice will enable you to rewire your neurological habits of your brain so as to access your confidence.

## Visualizing public speaking success

Begin seeing yourself presenting with confidence. It's important to note that your present perception of yourself and your abilities is a belief structure. So if you believe that you lack confidence then that's what you will experience unless the belief is changed. Remember that your actions and behaviors can help with altering your beliefs. To visualize speaking with success;

- You can close your eyes and imagine yourself breath in confidence while you exhale fear. Practice breathing in and imagine yourself walking with confidence within the room.

- See yourself engaging with the audience positively. See yourself speaking and the audience looking amazed at how smart and informed you are. Go through the entire speech with the same feelings.

- As you conclude your message, revert to yourself and think of how confident and powerful at public speaking you are. Look at the audience exuding excitement and thanking you for your words.

- This is the place where your confidence lives and it's your power to public speaking.

## Slay the inner critic

The inner critic is the negative inner dialogue that keeps popping with negative messages. It has a way of diminishing one's confidence in public speaking if you believe it. I could emerge from statements that you were once told such as "you sound terrible when you speak," "You have a bad accent" and such like. To overcome negative inner dialogue, you have to be aware of them. You can do the following;

- Focus on your past successes with public speaking even if you aren't experienced yet.
- Replace the negative inner dialogue with something positive and empowering.

## Develop a fearless stage persona

Confident speaking is not about imitating anyone or putting up an act, however it can still help with adopting a stage persona that enables one to stretch into the fearless parts of their being. To develop a persona that's fearless, you should ask yourself the following questions;

- What are the best qualities that you have as a speaker? Are you compassionate, focused, or cool? Are you great at change or a powerful peacemaker?

- What might your trademark features look like? What do you do with your hands as you speak? Are you slow and well calculated with your movements or more energetic as you move about the stage? Identify these unique internal traits then develop them and utilize them in making your public speaking confident and second to nature.

## Mix the ingredients up

Great public speakers have a mix of certainty and confidence that uniquely belongs to them. They are the actual creators of their confident speaking as the fearlessness is not given by anyone. They choose to build it by honing their skills through practice and preparation. Everyone has the ability to feel the sense of power and the deep confidence that comes with believing in your message.

# Chapter 3

# Speech Creation and Delivery

To become great at public speaking, one should have a clear understanding on how to create and deliver a speech. In public speaking context, creation of a speech refers to researching, organizing and outlining the information that you intend to present. Once you have created your speech, the next step is to work on delivery. Delivery is what determines whether one is a great speaker or not.

It's through delivery that you get to communicate your confidence and your level of preparedness to the audience. Effective delivery is what shows your audience that you have researched the topic well and you understand what you are talking about. As much as delivery is something that should be happening at the moment of expressing your speech, effective delivery needs to be laid before one step into the podium.

To create your speech, you should follow the below steps;

## Research and preparation

Take time and consider the audience that you are to speak to and ensure that the tone of your speech and information is appropriate for the audience. Put yourself in your audience shoes and think of what you may want the outcome of your presentation to be. Take time and gather as much information as possible on the topic you are to speak on.

## Overcome Anxiety

Speakers at times do experience anxiety in many ways such as shaking hands and legs, rapid speech, voice fluctuations and sweating amongst others. To effectively deliver your speech, you have to overcome anxiety. As a public speaker, your goal should not be focused towards eliminating any form of apprehension; you can use them to invigorate your presentation. Having apprehension may act as a motivation for you to prepare effectively. It can also make you have the alertness and energy that in turn makes your presentation to be interesting.

**Write your speech**

Planning is critical if you are to deliver a successful speech. Ensure that you plan what the opening and closing statements should be and how you intend to transition through the different phases of speaking. Here are steps you can follow as you plan your speech;

- Begin with an attention grabbing fact. It can be a rhetorical question, a quote or any relevant anecdote. The opening speech should be something that grabs the audience attention.

- Keep a positive attitude and tone and ensure that you take a short time.

- Tell the audience what the problem could be, propose a solution and the actions that the audience can take to help.

- Plan a conclusion that summarizes the main points then finish up with a motivating and strong appeal for action. Ensure that you inspire your audience.

**Practice**

It's through practicing that you will be able to know your speech so well so that you can speak naturally as you glance occasionally at the notes. One of the biggest mistakes that many people make is failing to rehearse their speech enough. If you intend to give a compelling speech that has the potential of inspiring the audience to listen to your call to action then you have to spend plenty of time in preparation.

Here are some tips for practicing;

- Practice your speech as many times and ensure you do it before a friend for feedback. You can read the content aloud either with a friend or to yourself then make adjustments until the structure starts to flow and sound natural and conveys the message.

- Speak clearly and add gestures, eye contact and movement for more impact. Just ensure that you remain relevant and natural with the movements. Practice the movements, props and body language until you are accustomed to the moves.

- Do a rehearsal with the actual outfit you intend to wear. You can invite a few friends and family to watch you give the presentation. Try to avoid sticking to the podium. It may act as a barrier between you and the audience. You can put the notes on it then try to walk around as you speak.

## Set the tone

Tone generally refers to the feeling or the mood that the speaker creates. A speaker's level of confidence, attitude and emotional state is generally revealed through the tone of voice. The tone of voice is therefore a powerful tool that enables the speaker to engage with the audience, charm and even encourage them to listen. There are times when the tone is set by the occasion, such as speaking in a wedding or a funeral may require different tones. Wearing a smile or a happy face as you get up to deliver your speech helps with setting the tone of friendliness and warmth.

If you look tense and serious then you also set a different tone and it could be one of discomfort and anxiety. Remember that you get to set the tone for your presentation long before giving the speech. The tone that you set should be in a way related to the speech you are about to make.

## Language style

As a public speaker, the language style that you use in giving your speech shapes your speaking style. The language style is the vocal part of your nonverbal communication and it refers to pace or speed at which you're speaking, the pitch of your voice and the volume. Style may also refer to the type of phrasing that a speaker uses and the effect it creates. You should speak in a clear and precise way that the audience can clearly understand what you're expressing. Avoid mumbling and use of language that complicates the sentences.

Improve your language style by steadying your breath and reflecting on your pace. You can also elevate your speaking style by incorporating metaphors, simile and hyperbole in your speech. You can also consider using parallelism, repetition and personification for a better understanding of your speech. Have a vivid imagery as you bring your point across.

## Put the visual aids together

Visual aids are important aspects of your speech and can help in making unfamiliar information to be more accessible to your audience. You can use power point presentations, charts, videos and even photos to get your point across. You can keep the following in mind as you prepare visual aids;

- The visual aids that you use should be simple and also colorful. You should however remember that color green and red may be difficult to read from a distance.

- Keep the text to a minimum otherwise your audience may be confused on whether to read or listen to you. Use of a few charts or slides can help your audience understand the message however too many slides can be distracting.

- Videos provide a powerful way of passing information and you can consider that as well.

## Handling Q&A

The way you handle questions and answer sessions can in a great way strengthen your credibility as you get to demonstrate your knowledge. The Q&A session also gives you the opportunity to clarify and also expand on your ideas. To handle the session effectively you can do the following;

- List down possible questions that the audience may have in reference to what you are presenting and prepare the answer as well.

- If anyone in the audience is becoming antagonistic or aggressive then you can simply say that you'd be happy to talk about the matter in greater depth afterwards as you have limited time and you need to address other questions. Never allow anyone to take control over the presentation.

## Vocal Preparation

For effective public speaking, you also need to pay attention to your vocal variety. Vocal variety refers to the variation in your tone, the speaking rate and pauses as you speak. You need to vary the way you speak so that you don't sound the same all through the presentation. It's the variation in your vocals that will keep your audience interested and engaged in your presentation.

Keep in mind the vocal projection and ensure that you speak loud enough so that your audience can hear you well. Making eye-contact is another way you can use to show engagement with your audience. Use eye contact to create your persona and it can also add some credibility to your presentation.

# Chapter 4

# 10 Simple Methods to Public Speaking Mastery

Public speaking is a crucial ability that people should consider mastering not only for the sake of giving powerful and memorable speeches, it can also improve one's chances to success in business. The ability to express thoughts in a more convincing, clear and concise way can make a huge difference in one's life regardless of what they are involved in. Here are the simple methods to public speaking mastery;

## Unleash the Inner Master

A great public speaking should have a combination of both mindset (internal) and behaviors (external) factors. If you possess all the right behaviors but lack the right mental attitude then your audience will notice the incongruence and the presentation may come out as fake. Great speakers begin with a strong self belief as they define the purpose of their speech and what they intend to achieve for both themselves and the audience. Even as you work on your oratory skills and impressive body language, ensure that your mindset is right with positive self talk.

## Practice the Art of Story Telling

Human minds are wired for stories and great public speakers use stories to grab the audience attention and hook them to the speech. People love listening to great stories and stories in a way have some hypnotic effect on those listening to it. People are more likely to forget important things in the speech but they may not easily forget the story you shared. The story however should be simple and also relatable. The story should also present a clear point of view if it's to be considered as effective.

Personal stories are considered to be great since they are credible and has the potential of inspiring action. Even as you tell the stories, remember that it's about the audience even if it's a personal story. Make the story to be clear and figure out how it can help the audience and why it's important. Your speech will not only be interesting but will equally empower and inspire your audience. Great speakers use storytelling in their presentation as a way of;

- Making important points in the speech memorable
- Establishing connection with the audience
- Introducing issues that may be controversial
- Shaping beliefs and raising levels of energy within the audience
- Motivating people to act

## Focus on the audience and ignite a conversation

When engaging in public speaking, it's important to know that you are not talking to a crowd but a group of individuals. Each person within the room expects you to connect with them, reach out and even impact them individually. So consider igniting a conversation, make eye contact and speak deliberately in different parts within the room. Try to speak to each individual's special concerns. Stay in the moment and be mindful of your audience, focus exclusively on their needs than on your desire to look good.

## Deliver Captivating Moments

To create an emotional appeal, you should speak from the heart. Whether you are delivering a humorous talk or telling a story with the potential of moving the audience and connecting with your speech, purpose to speak from the heart. Pay attention to your body language and the vocal cues. Great public speakers are always aware of their voice and body language. Ensure that you contrast the change in your tone and body language to reflect the emotion and importance of what you're saying.

## Grab attention and close with dynamic end

The first words that you get to speak when you start a conversation can either turn them off, send them to sleep or grab their attention. Start your speech with an attention grabbing statement knowing that you have just a few seconds to gain their attention. Instead of spending the first moments in thanking the hosts then flipping to your power point slides which automatically turns the audience off; consider starting with a quotation; a statistic or even ask a question. You can also tell a short story as you get started.

You can conclude your speech with a strong statement that your audience is likely to remember and a summary of your speech.

## Stick to 18-Minute Rule

The science behind the 18-minute rule has been proven to be effective for public speakers and is a common practice with TED speakers. Giving people too much information can result into cognitive backlog and the more information one is required to retain the more they are likely to forget. If you have to give a presentation for more than 18 minutes then you should have mechanisms of reengaging the audience frequently. You can allow the audience to ask questions, share videos or stories as a way of reengaging them.

## Engage all the 5 Senses

Great public speakers know how to connect, engage and also persuade their audience using the five senses. To be effective as a speaker engage your sight by making eye contact with as many individuals within the audience as possible. Activate hearing senses by playing music either at the beginning or end of the presentation. To engage the thought, you can ask a question that the audience can contemplate over. As for the speech, engage by telling stories that are relevant to the subject. Engage touch senses by greeting people either before the presentation or after as they join to get started. You can also engage touch sense by patting someone in the audience as you speak and remember to wear a smile.

## Study the Masters

One of the best ways that you can use to become a great speaker is by following leaders, those who have mastered public speaking. There are several videos of exceptional speakers online that you can use to improve your public speaking skills. You can determine your area of interest and fully immerse yourself into learning and researching about the field so as to emerge as an expert in the field. Follow thought leaders and strive to stay in touch with the latest trends.

## Let your personality shine through

Be true to yourself by showing your passion. Avoid imitating other people even if you love their style. Be authentic, conversational and energetic. When you express your passion and believe in your topic it will show to your audience. You will be able to establish greater credibility if you allow your personality to shine through. Your audience may also get to trust you if they perceive you to be real. You don't have to master all that you have learnt at once just grasp a few and keep putting them into action as you deliver your speech.

## Fail Forward

To be great in public speaking you should not shy away from failing. Trying not to fail may hinder you from succeeding as a great speaker. Great public speakers are known to take chances and also make calculated risks of reaching their audience and sharing ideas. Avoiding being on the spotlight just because you failed and choosing to stay in your safe place may only hinder you from becoming that great speaker. Begin by speaking in small meetings such as kid's events, small gatherings and church

To be great at public speaking, you need to keep learning and improving your public speaking skills. You can join famous organizations such as toastmasters as they help people learn on how to deliver great speeches. Members learn by rotating in giving speeches and they also receive feedback from the group. The organization also helps with creating some sense of accountability and a safe environment for practice.

# Chapter 5

## Developing Persuasion Skills

Every public speaking opportunity provides one with a chance to shine and a chance to build their profile and brand. Persuasive speaking entails winning people over by combining use of words and ideas to change people's mind. Persuasion involves directing, appealing to the thinking and guiding an individual or an audience. The goal of persuasion is to enable the audience to accept the idea, action or the information being shared by the speaker.

To be able to effectively persuade, you should have a good understanding of your audience. You should get some insight on their needs, wants and their desires in relation to your ability to fill the needs. Consider their view point and figure out what you would do if you were in their position. Let go of the expected outcome and focus on their best interest and how you can help them realize it. There are three elements to being persuasive as a public speaker and mastering them can enhance your persuasion skills;

## Ethos

Ethos entails the credibility or the character of the speaker. In order to be asked to give a speech, share your observations, thoughts or make a presentation publicly as a speaker, you should be expressing some level of knowledge and authority in the given area. Before you get to convincing your audience to take some action there are aspects of credibility that you should look into such as below;

- Does the audience express respect towards you?
- Does the audience believe in you being of good character?
- Does the audience see you as trustworthy?
- Does the audience view you as an authority in the area of your speech?

It's important to note that your audience should be able to see you in this light if you are to persuade them successfully.

## Logos

Logos is synonymous with making logical argument and it entails the logic behind the conclusions that are drawn by a speaker. To ensure that the speech is well understood by the audience it has to be conveyed in a logical, informative and clear manner. To ascertain whether your speech is logical, you can consider the following;

- Does the speech make sense?
- Is the speech based on statistics, facts, or evidence?
- Will the call to action lead to the expected outcome as desired?

## Pathos

Pathos entails the ability to create an emotional appeal or a connection between the speaker and the audience. The speech should have the potential of capturing and holding the audience attention and for that to happen the speaker should be able to create emotional connection with the audience. Emotional connection can be achieved in diverse ways such as sharing a story, anecdote, simile, analogy, metaphor and analogy. The message being shared should be linked to the emotional trigger in a way that ignites response from the audience. You should be aware of the feelings that your words evoke. Ask your words evoke love, fear, compassion, hate, contempt and such like.

## Conclusion

Congratulations and thank you for reading the book all through to the end. Now that you have insight on what it takes to become great at public speaking; you should take the necessary steps of putting into practice what you have learned. Follow the steps shared and the actionable tips and ensure that you should practice.

As shared in the book, it takes practice to become a great speaker, don't be discouraged with failure. Keep getting out and putting yourself into the spotlight as it will just be a matter of time before you start reaping the fruits. Whether you are already started with learning the art of public speaking or you are just considering it; **Public Speaking: 10 Simple Methods to Build Confidence, Overcome Shyness, Increase Persuasion and Become Great at Public Speaking** is a book that has been written with you in mind.

Make use of the information shared to hone your skills and remember to keep learning as you sharpen your skills. You will be amazed by the benefits once you master the art of public speaking.

Thank you and enjoy your journey of becoming a great public speaker!

# Thank you!

Before you go, I just wanted to say thank you for purchasing my book.

You could have picked from dozens of other books on the same topic but you took a chance and chose this one.

So, a HUGE thanks to you for getting this book and for reading all the way to the end.

Now I wanted to ask you for a small favor. **Could you please consider posting a review on the platform? Reviews are one of the easiest ways to support the work of independent authors.**

This feedback will help me continue to write the type of books that will help you get the results you want. So if you enjoyed it, please let me know! (-:

Lastly, don't forget to grab a copy of your Free Bonus book *"Bulletproof Confidence Checklist"*. If you want to learn how to overcome shyness and social anxiety and become more confident then this book is for you.

Just go to:

https://theartofmastery.com/confidence/

www.ingramcontent.com/pod-product-compliance
Lightning Source LLC
LaVergne TN
LVHW051911060526
838200LV00004B/83